Contents

STOCK MARKET

INTRODUCTION

Wouldn't you love to be a business owner without ever having to show up at work? Imagine if you could sit back, watch your company grow, and collect the dividend checks as the money rolls in!

This situation might sound like a pipe dream, but it's closer to reality than you might think. As you've probably guessed, we're talking about owning stocks . This fabulous category of financial instruments is, without a doubt, one of the greatest tools ever invented for building wealth.

 Stocks are a part, if not the cornerstone, of nearly any investment portfolio. When you start on your road to financial freedom, you need to have a solid understanding of stocks and how they trade on the stock market .

Over the last few decades, the average person's interest in the stock market has grown exponentially. What was once a toy of the rich has now turned into the vehicle of choice for growing wealth. This demand coupled with advances in trading technology has opened up the markets so that nowadays nearly anybody can own stocks. Despite their popularity, however, most people don't fully understand stocks.

Much is learned from conversations around the water cooler with others who also don't know what they're talking about. Chances are you've already heard people say things like, "Bob's cousin made a killing in XYZ company, and now he's got another hot tip..." or "Watch out with stocks--you can lose your shirt in a matter of days!" So much of this misinformation is based on a get-rich-quick mentality, which was especially prevalent during the amazing dotcom market in the late '90s. People thought that stocks were the magic answer to instant wealth with no risk.

The ensuing dotcom crash proved that this is not the case. Stocks can (and do) create massive amounts of wealth, but they aren't without risks. The only solution to this is education. The key to protecting yourself in the stock market is to understand where you are putting your money.

It is for this reason that we've created this tutorial: to provide the foundation you need to make investment decisions yourself. We'll start by explaining what a stock is and the different types of stock, and then we'll talk about how they are traded, what causes prices to change, how you buy stocks and much more.

What Are Stocks?

The Definition of a Stock : Plain and simple, stock is a share in the ownership of a company. Stock represents a claim on the company's assets , equity and earnings . As you acquire more stock, your ownership stake in the company becomes greater. Whether you say shares , or stock, it all means the same thing.

Being an Owner Holding a company's stock means that you are one of the many owners (shareholders) of a company and, as such, you have a claim (albeit usually very small) to everything the company owns. Yes, this means that technically you own a tiny sliver of every piece of furniture, every trademark, and every contract of the company. As an owner, you are entitled to your share of the company's earnings as well as any voting rights attached to the stock.

A stock is represented by a stock certificate. This is a fancy piece of paper that is proof of your ownership. In today's computer age, you won't actually get to see this document because your brokerage keeps these records electronically, which is also known as holding shares "in street name ". This is done to make the shares easier to trade. In the past, when a person wanted to sell his or her shares, that person physically took the certificates down to the brokerage. Now, trading with a click of the mouse or a phone call makes life easier for everybody.

Why Trade In Stock Market

• 1. You do not need a lot of money to start making money, unlike buying property and paying a monthly mortgage.

• 2. It requires very minimal time to trade -unlike building a conventional business

• 3. It's 'fast' cash and allows for quick liquidation (You can convert it to cash easily, unlike selling a property or a business).

• 4. It's easy to learn how to profit from the stock market easy to learn how to profit from the stock market . . But You need to have your basics clear. Unless you do….you will be wasting your time and loosing money.

You need to be crystal clear of each and every aspect of Investments , stock options, Stock Trading, Company, Shares Dividend & Types of Shares, Debentures, Securities, Mutual Funds , , IPO , Futures & Options, What does the Share Market consist of? Exchanges, Indices, SEBI , Analysis of Stocks –How to check on what to buy?, Trading Terms (Limit Order, Stop Loss, Put, Call, Booking Profit & Loss, Short & Long), Trading Options – Brokerage Houses etc.

Stock Market System

• Primary market

• stock market is a secondary market

• Trade stock for listed corporations trade stock for listed corporations

 • Progressive development of stock market

Primary Market

• The primary market provides the channel for sale of new securities. Primary market provides opportunity to issuers of securities; Government as well as corporate to raise resources to meet their requirements of investment and/or discharge some obligation.

• They may issue the securities at face value, or at a discount/premium and these securities may take a variety of forms such as equity, debt etc. They may issue the securities in domestic market and/or international market

Why Companies need to issue shares to Public

• Most companies are usually started privately by their promoter(s). However, the promoters' capital and the borrowings from banks and financial institutions may not be sufficient for setting up or running the business over a long term. So companies invite the public to contribute towards term. So companies invite the public to contribute towards the equity and issue shares to individual investors.

• The way to invite share capital from the public is through a 'Public Issue'. Simply stated, a public issue is an offer to the public to subscribe to the share capital of a company. Once this is done, the company allots shares to the applicants as per the prescribed rules and regulations laid down by SEBI.

Secondary Market

• Secondary market refers to a market where securities are traded after being initially offered to the public in the primary market and/or listed on the Stock Exchange. Majority of the trading is done in the secondary market.

Secondary market comprises of equity markets comprises of equity markets and and the debt the debt markets markets

• Difference between Primary and Secondary Market is In Primary Market securities are offered to public for subscription for the purpose of raising capital or fund Secondary Market is an equity trading venue in which already existing/pre-issued securities are traded among investors.

Equity Investment

• When you buy a share of a company you become a shareholder in that company. Shares are also known as Equities. Equities have the potential to increase in value over time. It also provides your portfolio with the growth necessary to reach your long term investment goals. Research studies have proved that the equities have outperformed most other forms of investments in the long term term ..

• Equities are considered the most challenging and the rewarding, when compared to other investment options.

• Research studies have proved that investments in some shares with a longer tenure of investment have yielded far superior returns than any other investment.

• However, this does not mean all equity investments would guarantee similar high returns. Equities are high risk investments. One needs to study them carefully before investing

Types of investors

 • Speculators

• Hedgers •

• Arbitragers

Important Jargons

o BSE Sensitive Index or SENSEX

 O Bull Market

O Bear Market

O Delivery

O Intraday

o Dematerialization

o Long Buy

o Short Selling

o Stop Loss

o Portfolio

o Tick Size

o Averaging

o Booking Profit or Loss

o Crash -Curciuts

o Right Issue

o Stock bonus

o Stock Split

All companies have owners.

 A small company started by a single individual may have only him or her as the single owner. The large corporations that have stock (shares that are traded by the general public) have many owners.

To simplify and organize the buying and selling of these shares by the general public, companies use the stock market. In fact, US government regulations require that a company, once it reaches a certain number of owners, must go public. This is to allow its now large number of owners to be able to buy and sell their shares of stock in the company more easily.

Just think about it this way. Let's pretend that your sibling or a close friend is starting a small company. He or she is doing really well, but needs more money (capital) to expand. He or she asks you to become a part owner in the business by investing some of your savings. You agree. Would you try to sell your ownership in the company just a few days later?

Most likely not! It should be the same thing when you decide to buy a public company's stock. The only real difference is that your sibling's or friend's company is a private company with just two shareholders, whereas there are many more owners in a public company with shares in the "stock market." "Without a saving faith in the future, no one would ever invest at all. To be an investor, you must be a believer in a better tomorrow" Benjamin Graham

ACTIVITY: FIND THE STOCK

 Investing in a stock is buying a piece of the company. Search the internet to match the brands with the company (stock) that owns it. What stock ticker (example AAPL for Apple) would you buy if you wanted to invest in the growth of the following products? ESPN , Pampers, YouTube

BEATING THE MARKET

To start, let me introduce you to Warren Buffett. Mr. Buffett has been the single most successful investor since the late 1950s. Let's set the stage. The year is 1984. Recently, there had arisen a growing consensus that the stock market was fully efficient, called "Efficient Market Theory." Basically, academics and investors were declaring it impossible for someone to consistently pick stocks that would beat the overall market average, because everything was priced in already.

Columbia Business School hosted an epic debate as a contest between Michael Jensen, a professor from the University of Rochester and one of the leading voices of the Efficient Market Theory versus Warren Buffett, famed stock-picker. Jensen went first.

He argued that if you flipped a coin 50 times, there would be someone that happened to get heads 50 times in a row, but that didn't mean that that person had skill. He called picking stocks a "coin flip". T hen Buffett spoke. He said "let's imagine that we had a coin f lipping contest. And that of course we could have some lucky winners and losers. But then, let's assume that all the winners had something in common.

What if all the winners of the coin-flipping contest came from Omaha, or had an unusual technique. Wouldn't you be curious to find out what made this high concentration of winners?

Buffett then went through the investment performance of nine successful investors that just so happened to all practice the same methodology and all had the same teachers, Benjamin Graham and David Dodd.   He called them "The Superinvestors of Graham-andDoddsville."

Buffett was unequivocally declared the winner after his masterful speech.   No one could doubt the numbers or the logic.   The clear conclusion is that you can be successful in picking stocks, and it requires following the investment principles of Graham and Dodd and Buffett.

THE SEVEN GOLDEN RULES

Being successful at anything requires following a set of rules. Good rules are the accumulation of decades of wisdom summed up into the few components that really matter. Successful football players win because they avoid penalties and because of the way they train. Successful students get A's because of the way they study.

Investing in the stock market is no different, except that when you succeed in investing you make money - a lot of money. Take Warren Buffett for example; he started out with $10,000 and turned it into a net worth of $60,000,000,000 (That's 60 BILLION!) . But he's not alone. Peter Lynch, Bill Ruane, Walter Schloss, Bill Miller, Charlie Munger, Joel Greenblatt, and many others generated similar extraordinary investment returns, consistently, over a long-term time horizon.

Each successful fund manager's style was slightly different, but if you study them each carefully you'll start to see significant patterns. We summed these patterns into Seven Golden Rules. So, without further ado,

Here are the Seven Golden Rules of Successful Investing so that you can crush it in the stock market.

RULE 1: THINK LONG-TERM

Trying to time the stock market or risking it all to "double your money in a year" is at best speculating, at worst gambling. You may as well just take your money to Vegas and lose it there. Those who are able to successfully navigate the stock market are not speculators or gamblers, they are investors.

 Investors know they can beat the market because they think differently, they think smarter, and they think longer-term. "Time horizon arbitrage" means that if investors learn to think long-term and can see beyond the daily and quarterly noise, they can gain a real upper hand. In 1964, American Express was a great company but the stock was getting hammered due to an insurance scandal.

The company had to pay millions of dollars in fines due to accidentally underwriting barrels of vegetable oil that turned out to be water. That is exactly the time when Warren Buffett began purchasing the stock. The best investors look beyond short term distress and keep their eyes on the long-term horizon. "Only buy something that you'd be perfectly happy to hold if the market shut down for 10 years." -Warren Buffett

RULE 2: GOOD COMPANIES MAKE GOOD INVESTMENTS

People need to understand that investing is not like placing a bet on whether the Cowboys will cover the spread against the Packers in the big game. Investing is not trying to get the quarterly press release a microsecond before the other person. It is not even about trying to predict which stock that you think will go up the most. Fundamental Investing is buying a tangible piece of a business, or a share of that business. And your investment portfolio (the collection of all the different shares you own) is only as good as sum of the companies in that portfolio. If you buy shares of high quality companies at reasonable prices, you'll end up with a high quality portfolio with less risk. It's as simple as that. Good companies are ones that have a unique advantage that others can't copy. Good companies are ones that generate high returns on capital. Good companies don't need to borrow a lot because their business is selff inancing. "It's far better to buy a wonderful company at a fair price than a fair company at a wonderful price" Warren Buffett

RULE 3: BUY WITH A MARGIN OF SAFETY

Nearly every professional investor began his career reading Benjamin Graham's, The Intelligent Investor. Warren Buffett called it, "by far, the best book on investing ever written." What makes it so special? One of the reasons is because it introduced the important concept "Margin of Safety."

In investing, a margin of safety is formed when one buys an investment at less than its value, while using conservative assumptions. The idea of a margin of safety is that you want to buy a business at a price that is low enough that your assessment could be completely wrong and you wouldn't lose much.

RULE 4: DO YOU OWN HOMEWORK AND OWN WHAT YOU KNOW

 T here is no substitute for your own work. Buying a stock because CNBC recommended it, or because your uncle recommended it, or the stock chart looks good is a sure way to lose money. Successful investors know what they own. They buy stocks of companies with products they believe in. Successful investors go the extra mile to analyze the financials of the company to make sure they're not missing anything.

Remember, most of the extraordinary gains made in the stock market come after a stock is punished or after it has already risen a lot, but you're not going to have the conviction to stick with it unless you really know the company. "You have to know what you own, and why you own it." -Peter Lynch.

RULE 5: DON'T FOLLOW THE HERD, STAY CALM AND RATIONAL

 T he typical buyer's decision is usually heavily influenced by those around him:

buy when others are buying, sell when others are selling. Unfortunately, this is a recipe that is bound to backfire.

The best investors are ones that can fight this urge and remain calm through a storm, and remain on the sidelines through a bubble. T he world's greatest investor Warren Buffett said it best, "Be fearful when others are greedy, and be greedy when others are fearful!"

RULE 6: DON'T PUT ALL YOUR EGGS IN ONE BASKET, BUT DON'T HAVE TOO MANY BASKETS, EITHER

Diversification is one of the most critical strategies for your portfolio so that if one stock blows up, it won't sink the entire ship. As much as we think we won't make a mistake, we will. Even the masters do and that is why we can't put all our eggs in one basket. T here's power in diversification.

However, research suggests that 90% of diversification benefits can be obtained in most markets with a portfolio of just over 20 stocks. The more you diversify beyond that, the less you know about each investment (See Rule #4). Your first and second best ideas are always better than your 100th best idea, so while diversifying is crucial, make your best ideas count!

RULE 7: NEVER STOP LEARNING

Perhaps the most important rule is learn, learn more, and then keep learning. The fun thing about investing is that the markets are always different and companies are constantly changing.

 Never stop learning about businesses, never stop learning from other great investors, and never stop learning from your own mistakes. Humility and an eagerness to learn are two traits found in all of the great investors. Even Warren Buffett credits his partner Charlie Munger with teaching him that it's better to buy a great company at a fair price than a fair company at a great price. "The game of life is the game of everlasting learning.   At least it is if you want to win."   -Charlie Munger

8TH BONUS RULE WHEN YOU MAKE A LOT MONEY, FIND MEANINGFUL WAYS TO GIVE IT BACK.

Bill & Melinda Gates took their fortune and lifted millions of people out of poverty through their foundation. Warren Buffett has done the same with his billions.   If you make millions or even billions of dollars through the concepts taught by YIS, we hope that you will take it and make the world a better place.   And even if you don't make millions, you can find important ways to give back to your community. Giving, can be done not only with money, but also with your time, your energy and your talents.   At YIS, we believe it's possible to really make our investments count.   That's why we're investing in you.

KEY TAKEAWAYS

Warren Buffet and many others made it clear that it is very possible to make exceptional returns from the stock market, following a few simple rules. Investing is simple, but it is not easy. The Golden Rules of Investing are widely known but difficult to follow in practice. By investing in a stock you are owning a portion of a business.

THE VALUE OF A STOCK

Introduction Imagine in front of you is a box of a dozen doughnuts. How much would you pay for one donut? If all the donuts in the box are the same, is one worth more than the other?

What if the world had a shortage of sugar and this was the last box of donuts in the world, with none being able to be made for the next year? Does the scarcity increase the value of the good?

How about if you just ate a box of donuts and can't eat any more, does the value you would pay for a donut decrease? T he box of 12 doughnuts represents a company. When you break the company down, everyone has an opportunity to own some of the donuts, or part of the company. But people may pay wildly different prices for the same donut. If you want to maximize the value of a box of donuts, what might be the best approach?

One method is to convince people that these are the tastiest donuts in the world and they will only be around for a limited time. In a nutshell, this is how the market works. The stock market is made up of people that get excited about something or sick of something depending on their mood. What is obvious is that occasionally the market goes nuts!

WHY DO STOCK PRICES FLUCTUATE SO MUCH?

Open any financial newspaper like the Wall Street Journal. Turn to the stock quote section, pick any company at random, and look at the high and low stock price from the past year. (or go to yahoo.finance) Ok, let's see here. We have GM. They make cars and trucks.

Over the past 52 weeks, their stock traded as low as $28/share and as high as $39/share. They have 1.6 billion (bn) shares outstanding, so that means that the market value of GM was as low as $45bn and as high as $62bn. That's a difference of $17 billion dollars in value.

 Now the car business doesn't really change that much. You sell plus or minus 5% more vehicles per year. Chevy Silverado is a Chevy Silverado and they're not figuring out how to replace gasoline for water, or how to fly to the moon. It's basically the same business this year as it was last year. So how in the world could the value fluctuate by $17 billion dollars?

And more so, why is this happening with every single company in the stock market? Was last year an exceptional year of price swings? Nope Is there something the market knows that we don't know? No. So, what's the explanation? Well, it can be summed up into four short words:

"THE MARKET GOES NUTS!" MR. MARKET

Let me tell you a story. It's a story that legendary investor Benjamin Graham told. It is about a business partner of yours, named Mr. Market. Imagine you own a business together. Now, Mr. Market is a good guy, but he suffers from wild mood swings. One day he wakes up, and the sky is blue and he is feeling really, really good. So he offers to buy out your stake in the business for way more than it is worth. Then the next day, he wakes up and it's raining, he's feeling desperate, and he is screaming that the world is going to end.

He offers to sell you all of his stock in the company for half of what you paid for it. You take it! The next day, Mr. Market offers to pay a price that is neither extraordinarily high nor extraordinary low, so you just do nothing. Now the value of the business didn't really change from day to day – what changed was the erratic moods of Mr. Market. In short, Mr. Market is one moody dude.

So does this mean that we shouldn't invest in the stock market, because of these wild swings in the short term? To the contrary! The fact that we are offered deals from time to time should make us very, very excited.

Our goal is to 1) identify what the company is worth and 2) to wait for Mr. Market to have a bad day and buy it at a large discount. Benjamin Graham called this giving ourselves a "margin of safety." This is the equivalent of buying dollars for fifty cents. Ok, you're thinking. This is all well and good. Wait for the market to go crazy and buy below the fair value.

However, there is one problem: How can we be sure that we can even come close to knowing the value of a company? How can we be sure that our forecasts (a.k.a. wild guesses) are even in the ballpark? Aren't there a ton of smart people and computer programs waiting to scoop up a bargain as soon as it becomes available? Surprisingly, not as many as you think.

QUESTION TO CONSIDER: 1. Think about something that you got a really killer deal on that you bought in the past, how were you able to get that deal? How is this similar to the stock market?

WHAT IS THE VALUE OF A BUSINESS?

We'll only invest in a company when the price we pay today is significantly less than the value we will get tomorrow. Example: Teacher picks a student at random. Teacher holds up a $10 bill and asks the student, "What is the value of this bill?" Ten dollars. Teacher holds up ten $1 bills. She asks the same question, "What is the value of these dollar bills?" Ten dollars. Teacher offers to sell the student the $10 bill for the ten $1 dollar bills. This is a wash so maybe he'll take it, maybe he won't. T hen Teacher offers to sell the $10 for only five $1 dollar bills. Of course he should take it. Ask the question to the rest of the class at large, "How many of you would buy this?" Do the reverse. Ask to sell the $10 bill for twenty $1 bills? How many would take this? None of them. T he best investors are able to snatch up $10 bills when the market is only asking $5 for them. But how is this possible? It ispossible because 1) the value is tricky to calculate and 2) the market is irrational.

Remember the Market goes nuts. Is this a good thing or a bad thing for you? It's a very good thing. If all investors based their investment decisions on rational and conservative estimates of intrinsic value, it would be very difficult to make money in the stock market.

Fortunately, the participants in the stock market are humans subject to the corroding influence of emotions. Many investors will give into hype around stocks, or people will hop on a trend, because they have optimistic views that they can beat the system. As young investor geniuses, we will always check emotions at the door and buy stocks based on what they are really worth. But how do we know what the value of the company is? Let's take Apple. What is the value of the world's largest business of consumer electronics? The value of any business is the present value of all future cash the company will make minus the cash it needs to invest to make this happen. Ok, that's a bit of a mouthful, stay with me.

Let's assume that today Apple sells 200 million (mn) products per year at an average price of $1,000 each. So they make $200 billion dollars a year in sales. But to make those 200mn products, they spend $700 per device to design and make them and $100 to buy the equipment.

So they're taking home $200 per device, or 40bn dollars. Would you pay $40 to receive $40 next year? No, not unless you think Apple is going to keep making money the following year. Ok, let's assume Apple sells 5% more products every year at the same price of $1,000.

Next year they make $44bn, the following year they make $48.4bn and so on. The value of Apple then becomes everything under the line. Let's assume Apple can keep this trend for the next 40 years.

The total amount of profits going forward, at today's value is about $675 billion dollars.

Not bad, eh? Divide that by the number of shares outstanding, and we have the value of the shares at about $111 dollars per share. Annual Profit Products sold 200 million X Average Price $1,000 each = Sales $200 billion - Product Cost $160 billion ($700 + $100 X 200 million)   Profit $40 billion (or $200 per device)

QUESTION TO CONSIDER:

1. How much profit would Apple make if it sold 500 million products per year at the same price and the same profit per device? Apple Financials, assuming that they sell 5% more devices per year at the same price: 20152016201720182019202020212022 2023 20242025CONT..Price1,000$ 1,000$ 1,000 $ 1,000$ 1,000$ 1,000$ 1,000$ 1,000$ 1, 000$ 1,000$ 1,000$ 1,000$ Sold (mn)200210220.52322432552682812953 10 326342Revenues200,000210,000220,50023 1,525243,101255,256268,019281,420295,491 310,266325,779342,068Cost   -$800-$800- $800-$800-$800-$800-$800-$800-$800- $800-$800- $800Profit$40,000$42,000$44,100$46,305

$48,620$51,051$53,604$56,284$59,098$62,053$65,156$68,414

Now let's tweak with the numbers. Let's say instead of growing 5% per year, Apple only manages to sell the same amount of devices every year going forward. The graph becomes flat and the total value of Apple is nearly cut in half to $391mn, or $64/share.

At the current share price that means you're going to lose half your money. Now, let's assume that Apple manages to have very strong growth of 15% per year for a few years, but in year four the company has competitive pressure and profits get cut in half. Then they get cut in half again and profits remain at this level going forward. The value of Apple plummets to $220bn or $36/ share. Ouch!

So first we have the market definition of what a company's value is and second, we have tips and tricks from other investor geniuses. The value of what a company is worth really rests on just two questions:

1) How much are profits going to grow and

2) How long are these profits sustainable? T hose are the two things that determine how much value comes back to you in the long run as an owner of the business. 'How long will this last?' is probably the most important question you can ask yourself, in trying to figure out what a company is worth.

Now, even the best investors will tell you they have been dead wrong on the value of companies on many, many occasions. They'll also admit to you that for half of the companies on the market, they frankly have no idea what the true value of the company is. Why? Because the future of many companies is too uncertain to predict. If you don't know how long those profits will last, you can't compute what the company is worth. For most companies it is a wild guess how long those profits can last because they don't have any real defenses.

They don't have an economic moat. The good news is that there are some exceptional companies with a substantial moat around their castle that we know can't be competed away easily. By investing in these high-quality businesses we can have much more assurance that they will have a good value today as well as tomorrow. T hese are the companies we can feel confident that we are at least in the right ballpark when calculating their long term value.

So when Mr. Market comes to us in one of his bad moods wanting to sell us shares of really great companies at a discount, we say, "Sure! Give me all you got!"

HOW DO I COME UP WITH INVESTMENT IDEAS?

Now, we're getting to the fun part - picking stocks. But where do we start? One common investment motto is to "invest in what you know." This is a good place to start, but we also need to be careful. Many companies we know are actually terrible investments. For example, let's go back 15 years. In the year 2000, what were the companies that the average person knew? We shopped at Sears every weekend, we surfed the internet on Netscape, we took pictures with Kodak film, we bought GM cars and we flew on Delta Airlines.

Alright, sweet! Load up a portfolio of the things we know! T he problem is that all five of those well-known companies would go bankrupt in the next decade and we would lose all our money.

Just because something is well-known, doesn't mean that it's a good business. Warren Buffett taught that we do indeed want to own simple, easy to understand businesses, but that these businesses need a competitive moat around them. The problem with all of the businesses we mentioned before is that none of them really had a protective moat around them. Sears was out-priced by

Wal-Mart, Netscape lost out to Microsoft Explorer, Kodak was uprooted by a change in the technology, GM's cars went out of favor, and Delta went bankrupt along with just about every other airline. (By the way, if you want a business that is good at torching piles of cash, airlines are always a good place to start!)

So how do we start finding truly good businesses? Remember back to Lesson 3 on Economic Moats.

Start by asking yourself a few questions:

❋ What products am I happy to pay a price premium for because the service they offer can't be replicated by another? (Brand, Quality)

❋ What services do I continue paying for because switching services would be too costly or a huge inconvenience? (High Switching Costs)

❋ What platform do I use because it is the only one where I can meet up with a certain type of people and because the network or marketplace can't even be compared to a peer? (Network Effect)

✿what products have been around for generations – you can picture your parents and grandparents enjoying them and easily picture your grandkids enjoying them as well? (Sustainability, Brand)

Legendary investor Peter Lynch, who averaged a 29% return per year over 23 years at Fidelity, tells the story of his wife coming home from the grocery store and mentioning a new product – pantyhose in an egg shaped case called "L'eggs." She raved about what good products they were.

He also noted that she was picking up more pantyhose than ever, because she was visiting the grocery store twice a week compared to the department store which she only visited maybe every other month. With this knowledge in hand, he began aggressively buying shares in Hanes, the maker of the L'eggs pantyhose. The stock became a 30-bagger for his fund, meaning it didn't just double or triple, it went up 30x! He found the idea, not from the Wall Street Journal, but from paying close attention to how people were using the products around him. Peter Lynch's legendary book One Up on Wall

Street is a great resource to see how one of the most successful investors of his time came up with some of his best investment ideas.

ACTIVITY: CAN'T LIVE WITHOUT IT

Make a list of three companies that have products that you "can't live without" considering the questions above. Do youthink this company could make a good investment?

STOCK SCREENS

Another useful way to search out great stocks is to run a stock screen. Basically, when you run a stock screen you are running the stock market through a giant filter to sort out the characteristics that you want. It's similar to choosing a car: you know you want a blue, four-door car with good gas mileage, at a certain price, with a minimum horsepower. You put all this info into a search engine and come out with your "Goldilocks" car.

The concept is similar for a stock screener. When you know what to look for, a stock screen is a wonderful starting point. T hese are some of the financial characteristics that you should screen for among your initial list of investment candidates. Ideally you want to find a great company that is growing and you can buy cheap.

Here are a couple of factors you can look for:

❀ A business that has very stable earnings, with little fluctuation year to year

❋A company that has positive cash generation (Cash generation is the cash profits minus the investment costs to grow the business.)

❋ A company that consistently makes a healthy return on capital

❋ A company that pays a dividend that grows consistently every year One of the most popular (and free!) stock screeners out there is Google's.

Google's Stock Screener allows you drag the range for a number of different criteria. It also allows you to go to "Add Criteria" and customize what you want to screen. T here are many different metrics to screen for, but here are some helpful starting points: (If you see terms you don't recognize below, refer to the glossary at the end of this page or investopedia.com) Go to Google Stock Screener and start playing around with the following screens.

IS THE COMPANY GOOD?

❀ 5y Return on Equity: greater than 12% (Also use Return on Investment)

❀ Good companies often have high margins (Gross Margin > 30%, Operating Margin > 15%)

❀ Interest Coverage above 3 times

❀ Stable earnings and Return on Equity through the years (look at a chart, or look over the past 10 years, on Morningstar.com or zacks. com) IS THE COMPANY GROWING?
❀ 5y revenue growth greater than 4% per year

❀ 5y earnings growth (and EPS) greater than 4% per year

❀ Forecasted growth in the next 5 years IS THE STOCK CHEAP?

❀ P/E ratio below 15x (market average)

❀ Dividend yield above 3%

❀ P/Book ratio below 2x

Note, just because a company doesn't meet all of these thresholds does not automatically mean that the company is not a good investment. A very high quality company that is growing and that is very cheap is ideal, but is very rare. If you're trying to buy a new Ferrari under $10,000 you aren't likely to find many results. Tradeoffs will often need to be made, but the best investors stay disciplined and find the best combinations.

Additional Stock Screening Tools: T here are many free stock screening tools available online. Other useful screeners are Zacks.com (screenshot in on the right), Yahoo Finance, GuruFocus (subscription required) and Uncle Stock. As you learn more about the stock market and read stories of successful investors, pay attention to what metrics they examine. For example, some successful investors look for high growth companies (companies growing more than 20% per year) that also have high margins (gross margin above 50%). T hese would be considered growth investors. Other successful investors look for very cheap companies (Price / Book below 1x).

These would be considered deep-value investors.

There are many ways to successfully invest, and screening helps give you a great starting point.

THE S&P 500 & THE DOW JONES:

One more list that is helpful is the Dow Jones Industrial Average. These are 30 of the largest and most significant companies in the United States. T here will be many companies on this list that you will know, and these are companies that have been leaders for decades and even centuries, such as IBM, Procter & Gamble and Nike. Next you could look at the S&P 500.

Here you will find a list of 502 companies (not exactly 500, some companies are listed twice!) that represent the largest, most common companies in the United States. As you scan through these lists you can think to yourself:

❀ Does that sector look interesting?

❀ Do I know and like this company's products?

❀ Do I have certain expertise about this company's products that would give me an edge?

❀ Do I expect this company to grow? Or just click on a company randomly and see where it takes you. You might find your treasure.

RESEARCH REPORTS:

One of the best sources of investment ideas is other investors! Remember, there's no rule in investing that says you can't own a stock that another person owns. Cherry picking is encouraged! One way to find ideas is to read blogs or reports on stocks. Also, successful investment managers publish quarterly investment letters where they describe their top holdings and why they own them.

Here are a couple of places to start reading:

✸**Seeking Alpha:** Seekingalpha.com is an excellent databank of investor reports on companies. Some of the writers are professional investors, some are not, but there is a plethora of articles written on companies, both large and small.

✸ **SumZero:** Similar to Seeking Alpha, sumzero.com is an online platform where investment professionals write investment reports and promote stock ideas.

✸ **Wall Street Journal and The Financial Times:** These are the two newspapers that every needs investor reads each day. Most people need to pay for online access, but you can read the articles for free if you copy the article's title into Google and access it through Google directly (a legal and very useful trick!).

❀ **Motley Fool:** Fool.com is an always-interesting mix of financial news, investment strategies, and large doses of humor balanced by hard hitting serious news and opinion. Tom and Dave Gardner and their talented staff have been delivering their unique and informed message since 1993 and the Fool is now a full-service financial media enterprise. If you'd like your investing information tinged with some pleasant sarcasm and edgy laughs, the Fool might be perfect for you.

❀ **Jim Cramer:** The host of CNBC's Mad Money and co-founder of T heStreet.com is a journalist, lawyer, and "infotainer" (his term). He's been dispensing financial and investment information to anyone listening since the mid-1990s.

If you need a break from reading financial statements or waiting for your stock screener to advise you on your next hot investment, Cramer might add some zest to your day. A former hedge fund manager, Cramer has been in the investment trenches for some time. You may not agree with all that he says, but you will be informed and entertained.

GuruFocus:

GuruFocus.com tracks the stock trades of successful investment managers to see what they are buying and selling. It also provides stock recommendations based on different investment criteria and has a robust stock screening tool.

❋ **Value Investors Club:** Valueinvestorsclub.com is an online investment club where top investment managers come together to share their best stock ideas.

❋ **Beyond Proxy:** Beyondproxy.com is one of the most successful investment blogs. It compiles interviews with portfolio managers and stock reports. Beyond this list, there are literally thousands of investor blogs out there. Some are good, some are not, and a few are truly excellent. The point is that there are many free sources available to provide thoughts on companies and the market.

GIVING DUE DILLIGENCE ITS DUE

 Once we come up with a list of a few interesting companies to potentially invest in, it's time to roll up our sleeves and kick the tires. Remember that buying a stock of a company is really like buying a piece of that company – you are becoming a company owner! You would not make such a big decision before carefully considering your investment.

Would you? It is funny that people often spend more time researching a movie to see or carefully studying the specs of a piece of electronic equipment they are planning to purchase than when buying a piece of their own company! In the early stages of the investment process, it is particularly useful to use the company's products f irst-hand.

Learn as much as you can about the company in which you are going to invest. Here are a couple of steps to think about when doing your company "due diligence" (as the pros call it). Make sure the company is actually investible, or publicly traded. You can search for companies' stock tickers on Yahoo Finance, or Morningstar.com. Go to the company website, click on the "Investor Relations" tab, and f ind a recent company presentation.

This will give you an overview of the business. Read through the more in-depth Annual Report, also on the company website. Sections to focus on are the Management Discussion & Analysis and the Segment Reporting.

Read other investors' opinions on the company on resources such as seekingalpha.com. Look through the company's financials on sites like Morningstar.com. Evaluate the trends of the main company metrics. Remember our Golden Rule #3, DO YOUR OWN HOMEWORK.

As you follow these steps and use all the resources available to you to do your detective work, you will begin to know the company inside and out. Remember, great investors see things that others don't. They think outside of the box. They do their own work and develop a conviction in their investments. T he stock market "aggregates" or adds up all the opinions and knowledge of market participants to come up with what the "consensus" (or the general market) thinks a company is worth at any given point in time. Some people will just follow the crowd and invest along with this consensus. But as a wise investor who has done your own homework, you will have a strong sense of how the company is likely to perform in the future and you can take advantage of the "misunderstandings" that take place in the stock market every single day. Scary news headlines may motivate other (perhaps less knowledgeable or prepared) investors to panic by selling the stock. If you feel you got a great price on a stock you bought for the long-term, you are more likely to hold on to it through thick and thin. In our experience, this is almost always the right thing to do with the stocks of great companies. Here it is worth making a distinction between great companies and great stocks. In some cases, and especially in the short term, these may not always be the same thing. However, in the long run, since stocks are no more than pieces of companies, great companies are really great stocks.

QUESTIONS TO CONSIDER:

1. What does it mean to be a shareholder of a company?

2. How is it possible to believe in a company or know it so well that you are confident that you are right and the market is wrong about what it is worth?

3. Why does the market get it wrong sometimes? After completing this lesson, you should start to use the skills you learned in Lessons 1-4 to make a list of companies you came up with by doing

some detective work. You start out with products you know and like, but gather additional evidence by seeing what other consumers are doing. You begin to run your own stock screens.

You know that by buying a stock, you become a part owner of the company that issued that stock. You know that it is important to really understand the company so that you feel more comfortable trying to predict its future. You are now ready to go to the next step. You need to narrow your list to the stocks you really want to buy (the companies in which you want to be an owner). And you're learning how to hunt for treasure!

KEY TAKEAWAYS:

1. Finding great stocks is like a treasure hunt, a very, very rewarding treasure hunt.

2. Invest in what you know and do your homework.

 3. Stock screens can be a powerful way to identify good companies.

4. Remember, there's no rule in investing that says you can't own a stock that another person owns! Reading research reports can be a great way to learn more about investing.

HOW DO I FORECAST REVENUES OF A COMPANY?

In its simplest form, future revenue can be calculated by multiplying the average selling price of the company's product by the number of expected products sold. However, forecasting revenue isn't that simple and can involve considering many different factors.

For instance, Apple would see increased revenue if it sold its iPhone for more money per unit, but only if the number of phones sold didn't decrease as a result of the price increase.

Apple would love for both the price per unit and the number of units sold to increase, but these two things can move in opposite directions as people tend to buy fewer units as the price of that unit increases. Apple can also increase the number of units sold by expanding geographically. If it were to begin selling phones in a new country it hadn't previously sold in, that would add revenue. There can be other offsetting factors too, however.

When Apple first introduced the iPhone, iPods were quite popular, but when people began to buy iPhones, which included integrated digital music players, they began buying fewer iPods. This effect made it so that while Apple gained lots of revenue from the sale of its iPhones, it began losing its normal iPod revenue. Companies can also gain additional revenue by taking market share from competitors.

If, for instance, the number of smartphones sold in the world is 1.2 billion per year and Apple sells 50% of those this year and 60% next year, it will see a revenue increase, all else being equal. This means Apple sold 600 million phones (50% of 1.2B) this year and will sell 720 million phones (60% of 1.2B) next year. This is known as "taking market share," as Apple essentially took a bigger piece of the pie by going from 50% of the market to 60% of the market. Another way a company can grow revenue is by being in a market where the market itself is growing. For instance, if the market (i.e., the number of smartphones sold) grew by 10% from 1.2 billion phones to 1.32 billion phones, even if Apple retained a 50% market share, it would still sell 10% more phones. Companies can also grow revenues through opening or building new stores, acquiring other companies, etc. To forecast the revenues of a company, one must evaluate the industry, the company, and its competitors.

Looking at a company's revenue growth rate for many years is a good start. However, you must be careful not to assume that an abnormal period of time is in fact normal. For instance, Apple's revenue growth rate was well over 10% per year since the early 2000s, and it even reached rates of over 50% after the company released the iPhone and iPad, but by 2013 Apple was a very large company with no new products in a long time, resulting in a growth rate of under 10% for the year. Had the analyst assumed that the company would grow revenue at 50% a year for countless years to come, he/she would've been in for a rude awakening. In conclusion, forecasting revenue involves a lot of different variables, but a savvy analyst who has done his/her homework should be able to generate a good forecast in time.

ACTIVITY: FORECAST REVENUES

Chose a company that is on your list from Lesson 4 that you can up with from screens or from a grocery store visit, or from other sources:

❀ How fast has this company been growing revenues over the past 5 years?

❀ How fast did this company grow revenues last year?

❀Has this company been growing faster or slower than its competitors?

❀What do you expect they will grow at over the next 5 years? Use resources such as Morningstar.com, Zacks.com and Yahoo.Finance to research these metrics.

HOW DO I FORECAST MARGINS OF A COMPANY?

When analyzing stocks, you will likely review the income statement, balance sheet and statement of cash flows. The income statement provides a f inancial summary of the operating results of the firm over a period of time such as a quarter or year. The first section of the income statement shows gross margins, simply the total revenue (sales) minus the cost of goods sold.

Financial companies and service-oriented companies tend to have high gross margins since they often have lower costs of goods sold. Whereas industrial and manufacturing companies have lower gross margins as they have high cost of goods sold. Does the car manufacturing company Toyota have high or low gross margins? That's right they have low gross margins! Car manufacturing has one of the higher cost of goods sold out of any industry, one car is made up of thousands of parts.

 Adding up all those parts equals a high cost of goods sold and lower gross margins. Remember the gross margin is simply subtracting the cost of goods sold from the total revenue. Which can be helpful when looking at two companies in the same industry, take Apple versus Samsung.

T hey both make wonderful cellular phones, who would you guess has higher gross margin? A. Samsung B. Apple

Apple has the higher gross margin and why is that important?   Whether they charge a higher price or they have lower cost of goods sold can lead to competitive advantages over the long run. Going a step further on the income statement you will notice operating incomes or EBIT.   Operating Income divided by total revenues is Operating margin.   Operating margin is a measure of profitability, how much of each dollar of revenue is left over after both cost of goods sold and operating expenses.

The operating expenses include payroll, sales commissions, marketing, transportation, travel, rent and other general expenses.   It's likely easier to comprehend if you think about buying a pair of pants. You are in the mall and want to buy a pair of pants that costs $50, that's a nice pair of pants right? They felt so nice you go ahead and buy them, did you know it only cost $20 to make those pants. That's the cost of goods sold right, $20. Did you pay too much? Let's think about it.

After the company made the pants, they had to ship the pants to the store by semi-truck, someone had to unload the shipment of pants, the company pays rent to have a store in the mall, the store has employees who put the pants on display and sold them to you, a commercial was made to promote the pants and these operating expenses add up to $25 on top of the $20 cost of goods sold. Leaving the company with a profit of $5 or gross operating margin of 10%.

GROUP ACTIVITY: MARGIN MATCHING

Let's play a matching game! Match the company with the operating margin they make: Walmart and Facebook. Company A has operating margin of 24% Company B has operating margin of 5% Hint, the secret behind Walmart is they offer the lowest prices and while they make little profit per good sold, they make up for it because they sell so much more socks, shampoo, and cereal than any of their competitors.

Match the operating margin to the following three companies, Coca-Cola, Nike and Boeing. Company A has operating margin of 8% Company B has operating margin of 13% Company C has operating margin of 25%

COMPANIES:

1). Amazon.com (ticker AMZN)– the largest eCommerce website in the world. Fast growing company, also has kindle, Amazon Fire and cloud storage business. Because of fast growth phase, the company is currently not profitable.

2). Coca-Cola Company (ticker KO) – The largest beverage company in the world. Coca-Cola is a high margin and high return (ROE) business (above 20%). Revenue has declined a bit in the past two years

3). Celldex Therepeutics (ticker CLDX) – an early stage biotech company working on an experimental brain cancer vaccine.

The company is spending significantly on research and development, but will not reap the rewards of this investment until many years down the road.

 4). Freeport McMorran (FCX) – One of the largest copper and gold miners in the world. The business has been hit due to declines in the prices of gold and copper.

They also own some oil and gas fields.

5). Costco (COST)– Costco is one of the largest retail chains in the US, operating a warehouse model that charges a membership fee. Inventory management and increasing sales per assets (sales turnover) is an important part of the business

6). Facebook (FB) – Facebook is the largest social network in the world. T he company has few real assets (buildings, equipment) and the bulk of their costs are employees. The company is in a high growth phase.

CONCLUSION

Is your head ready to explode yet? You probably feel a lot like you did in your first week of Spanish class. A little lost with a splitting headache. But give it a bit of time and you're well on your way to being able speak the language of finance.

Whether you become a world-famous stock investor in the future, an accountant, or maybe just a dentist trying to keep the records of the business, learning to read financial statements is critical. The more fluent you are, the more successful you will be in almost any industry of business.